Read This Book!

By Jordan Townsend.

Hope.

Summary: People find themselves homeless for the first time and try to navigate the challenges of finding immediate shelter and a safe place to sleep.

Step 1: Assess your immediate surroundings

- Take a moment to evaluate your current location and look for potential areas that could provide temporary shelter.

- Look for alcoves, doorways, parks, or other hidden spots that could offer some cover from the elements.

Step 2: Look for public facilities or community resources

- Identify nearby public facilities such as **24-hour transit stations, libraries, or community centers** that might have shelter options or resources available.

- Check whether any
local organizations or
religious institutions
offer temporary
shelter or support
services.

Step 3: Contact
homeless shelters or
helplines

- Look up homeless
shelters or crisis
hotlines in your area

and call them for
assistance.

- Explain your
situation and inquire
about available
emergency shelter
options.

Step 4: Utilize
smartphone apps or
websites

- There are
smartphone apps

and websites specifically designed to help find shelter for the homeless. Utilize these resources to locate the nearest available shelters or temporary housing options.

Step 5: Reach out to friends, family, or support networks

- Contact people you trust, such as friends, family, or support networks, to seek temporary accommodation or ask for their guidance in finding shelter.

Step 6: Consider nearby safe public spaces

- If all else fails, research safe public

areas where you can sleep for the night, such as well-lit parks, 24-hour cafes, or shopping centers that permit overnight stays.

Chapter 1: First Night on the Streets - Ensuring Safety during Sleep

Step 1: Stay in well-lit areas

- When choosing a spot to sleep, prioritize well-lit areas to reduce the risk of potential dangers.

- Aim for places near streetlights, busy areas, or within view of security cameras.

Step 2: Keep a low profile

- While sleeping in public spaces, it's important to maintain a low profile to avoid drawing attention.

- Use blankets or clothing to conceal your belongings and avoid displaying any valuable items.

Step 3: Secure your belongings

- Keep your belongings close and secure while you sleep.

- Consider using a lockable backpack or storing your valuables in a discreet bag to deter theft.

Step 4: Stay aware of your surroundings

- Develop a habit of being alert and aware of your environment.

- Take note of nearby exits, emergency contact points, or areas with higher foot traffic that might provide additional safety.

Step 5: Be cautious of strangers

- Trust your instincts and be cautious of strangers who approach you during the night.

- Remember that not everyone has good intentions, so it's essential to prioritize your safety.

Step 6: Regularly change sleep locations

- To minimize the risk of becoming a target for criminal activities, change your sleep location regularly.

- This will make it less likely for someone to identify your pattern or intentions.

Remember, this is a challenging situation, and seeking long-term housing solutions should be a priority. Reach out to local organizations specializing in homeless support to explore options beyond immediate shelter. Stay hopeful and resilient, and know that there are resources available to help you navigate through this difficult time.

Summary: Exploring various options for finding food, including soup kitchens, food banks, and local organizations that provide meals for the homeless.

Step 1: Research local soup kitchens, food banks, and organizations

- Use the internet to search for soup kitchens, food banks, and organizations in your area that

provide meals for the homeless.

- Look for ones that specifically focus on providing hope through food assistance.

- Take note of the location, contact information, and hours of operation for each option.

Step 2: Call or visit the soup kitchens

- Start by contacting the soup kitchens you found during your research.

- Ask about their services, including how often they provide meals, what their requirements are, and if they have any specific programs focused on hope.

- Take note of the information they provide to help you make an informed decision.

Step 3: Reach out to local food banks

- Contact the food banks you found in your research.

- Inquire about their available food

assistance programs and whether they have any programs aimed at promoting hope through providing meals.

- Ask if they require any documentation or proof of need to access their services.

- Make note of the information provided by each food bank to compare your options later.

Step 4: Explore local organizations

- Look into any local organizations or community centers that provide meals for the homeless or those in need.

- Find out if they have any specific programs or initiatives focused on spreading hope through food assistance.

- Determine if they have any additional services or resources that could benefit you in your search for food.

Step 5: Compare and evaluate your options

- Take a moment to review the information you gathered from soup kitchens, food banks, and local organizations.

- Consider factors such as proximity, frequency of meals, program requirements, and any additional support they offer.

- Weigh the benefits of each option and choose which ones best align with your needs and preference for promoting hope through food assistance.

Step 6: Make a plan and take action

- Once you have decided on the soup

kitchens, food banks, and organizations that you believe will best serve your needs, create a plan to access their services.

- Determine the schedule and any requirements for each option and make sure you understand how to access the food they provide.

- Take the necessary steps to attend the soup kitchens or food banks during their operating hours.

- Follow through on your plan consistently to ensure you have a reliable source of nourishment while maintaining a positive outlook on your situation.

Remember, this chapter in your journey focuses on finding food and promoting hope. Stay resilient and hopeful as you explore these various options.

Summary: Seeking temporary shelter in emergency shelters, shelters specifically for women or families, and understanding eligibility criteria.

**Step 1: Gather information about

emergency shelters
in your area

- Conduct online
research or contact
local government
agencies to find out
about emergency
shelters available in
your area.

- Make a list of
shelters that offer
temporary
accommodation for
individuals or
families in need.

Step 2: Determine eligibility criteria

- **Visit the websites or contact the emergency shelters on your list to learn about their eligibility criteria.**

- **Note down any specific requirements they may have, such as age limits, gender restrictions, or**

documentation needed.

Step 3: Identify shelters specifically for women or families

- Look for shelters that are specifically designed to accommodate women or families if applicable.

- Make a separate list
of these shelters to
consider based on
your needs.

Step 4: Assess your immediate shelter needs

- Evaluate your
personal
circumstances and
determine the type
of shelter that would

best meet your immediate needs.

- Consider factors such as safety, privacy, the presence of children, and any specific requirements you may have.

Step 5: Contact and inquire about availability

- Call the emergency shelters you have listed to inquire about their availability.

- Ask any questions you may have about the shelter, including how to apply for their services.

Step 6: Follow the application process

- If you find a shelter that meets your criteria and has availability, follow their application process.

- Fill out any necessary forms or provide required documents as instructed.

- Be prepared to provide personal information and

details about your situation.

Step 7: Seek assistance from local organizations

- If emergency shelters are not available or suitable for your needs, reach out to local organizations or non-profits that may be able to provide alternative shelter options.

- They can often provide guidance, support, or resources to help you find temporary accommodation.

Step 8: Prepare for your stay

- Once your application is

accepted, prepare for your stay at the shelter.

- Pack essential personal items such as clothing, toiletries, important documents, and any necessary medication.

- Follow any instructions provided by the shelter regarding check-in

procedures, rules,
and regulations.

Step 9: Follow up on
long-term housing
options

- While staying at the
emergency shelter,
use the opportunity
to explore long-term
housing options.

- Seek assistance
from housing

agencies, social workers, or local organizations that specialize in helping individuals or families secure permanent housing.

Step 10: Maintain hope and reach out for support

- Remember that seeking shelter in an emergency situation

can be challenging, but it's important to maintain hope.

- Reach out to supportive friends, family, or counselors who can provide emotional support during this difficult time.

- Stay proactive in your search for long-term housing and take advantage of any resources or assistance available to you.

Remember, every situation is unique, and these steps are just a general guide. It is important to adapt them to your specific circumstances and seek additional guidance or support as needed.

Summary: Tackling issues of domestic violence or abuse, seeking help from local organizations, hotlines, and support groups.

Introduction:

Facing domestic violence or any form of abuse is challenging, but

there is always hope for a better future. In this chapter, we will guide you through the steps to overcome abuse and seek relief. By reaching out to local organizations, hotlines, and support groups, you can find the support you need.

Step 1: Recognize the Abuse

1. Assess the situation: Identify the signs of abuse, such as physical harm, emotional manipulation, isolation, or control.

2. Reflect on your experiences: Recognize and acknowledge that what you have been experiencing is

abuse. Trust your instincts and seek validation from others if needed.

Step 2: Prioritize Your Safety

1. Create a safety plan: Determine a safe place to go to in case of emergency, such as a trusted friend or family member's home.

Prepare a bag with essential items, such as identification documents, money, clothes, and important phone numbers.

2. Secure your personal information: Protect your sensitive information by changing passwords and limiting access to your accounts. Consider informing

your workplace or school about the situation and providing them with a photo of the abuser if necessary.

Step 3: Reach Out to Local Organizations

1. Research local organizations: Look for reputable organizations that specialize in

domestic violence or abuse issues. Check for services offered, such as counseling, legal aid, emergency shelters, or support groups.

2. Reach out to them: Contact the organizations via phone, email, or their website. Explain your situation, express the need for assistance, and ask

about their available support programs.

Step 4: Utilize Hotlines and Helplines

1. Find helpline numbers: Look for national or regional helplines dedicated to helping victims of abuse. These hotlines are often available 24/7 and provide

confidential support and advice.

2. Dial the helpline: Call the helpline number when you are in a safe, private space. Explain your situation, ask for guidance, and inquire about local resources or support groups.

Step 5: Seek Support from Support Groups

1. Search for local support groups: Look for support groups specializing in overcoming abuse. These groups provide a safe space to share experiences, receive emotional support, and learn coping strategies.

2. Attend support group meetings: Join a support group either in-person or virtually, depending

on availability and your comfort level. Engage with others in the group, listen to their stories, and offer support to one another.

Conclusion:

By following these steps and utilizing the available resources, you can take proactive measures to overcome abuse and seek relief. Remember, seeking help requires courage, but in doing so, you can find hope and create a better future for yourself. Stay strong and prioritize your well-being.

Summary: Strategies for finding affordable or free clothing options, including secondhand stores, clothing banks, and donation centers.

Step 1: Research Secondhand Stores in Your Area

- Use search engines or online maps to find local

secondhand stores in your area.

- Look for stores that offer affordable or discounted clothing options.

Step 2: Visit Secondhand Stores

- Make a list of the stores you found during your research.

- Plan a day to visit these stores and allocate enough time for browsing.

- Dress comfortably and bring a reusable bag to carry any items you purchase.

Step 3: Explore Clothing Banks

- Research clothing banks in your

community that
provide free clothing.

- Determine the
eligibility criteria for
accessing these
services.

- If you meet the
criteria, make a note
of their location and
hours of operation.

Step 4: Contact
Donation Centers

- Look for local donation centers that accept clothing donations.

- Contact these centers to inquire about any clothing available for free or at a low cost.

- Ask about specific requirements or criteria for accessing clothing donations.

Step 5: Community Outreach and Organizations

- Reach out to local community outreach programs or organizations that provide assistance to individuals in need.

- Inquire if they have any programs or resources for acquiring clothing.

Step 6: Plan Your Scavenging Strategy

- After gathering information about the different options available, create a plan that suits your needs.

- Decide which stores, banks, or centers you want to visit first based on their offerings and accessibility.

Step 7: Gather Transportation and Supplies

- Ensure you have reliable transportation to get to the various locations.

- Bring a list of the necessary sizes or types of clothing you need.

- Carry enough cash or a payment method to make purchases if necessary.

Step 8: Visit Secondhand Stores and Clothing Banks

- Begin by visiting the secondhand stores on your list.

- Take your time to search through the racks and try on any potential clothing items.

- Consider any discounts or sales that might be available.

Step 9: Explore Clothing Banks and Donation Centers

- Once you have finished with the secondhand stores, visit the clothing banks or donation centers you identified.

- Follow their procedures for accessing free or low-cost clothing.

- Be respectful of any guidelines or rules they have in place.

Step 10: Evaluate Your Finds

- After visiting the various locations, assess the clothing items you have acquired.

- Consider if they meet your needs and preferences.

- Take note of any additional clothing

items you might still require.

By following these steps, you can strategically scavenge and find essential clothing items in an affordable or free manner, bringing hope to your wardrobe.

Summary: Exploring organizations, churches, and community centers that accept donations for the homeless, including clothing, household items, and personal hygiene products.

Step 1: Research local organizations, churches, and community centers

- Begin by searching online for organizations, churches, and community centers in your area that are known for accepting donations for the homeless. Look for ones that specifically mention accepting clothing, household items, and personal hygiene products.

Step 2: Make a list of potential donation centers

- Create a list of the organizations, churches, and community centers you have found that accept donations for the homeless. Include their contact

information and
location.

Step 3: Call the donation centers

- Start by calling the organizations, churches, and community centers on your list to confirm if they are currently accepting donations. Some centers may have specific days or hours when they accept donations, so it's important to check before planning your visit.

Step 4: Organize your donations

- Gather the clothing, household items, and personal hygiene products you wish to donate. Ensure that the items are clean, in good condition, and packaged appropriately if needed.

Step 5: Schedule a donation drop-off

- Once you have confirmed with a donation center that they are currently accepting donations, schedule a time and date to drop off your donations. Some centers may have designated drop-off areas or times specifically for donations.

Step 6: Prepare your donations for drop-off

- Before heading to the donation center, pack your donations in boxes or bags that are easy to transport and handle. Label them if necessary, and double-check that everything is securely packed.

Step 7: Deliver your donations

- Drive to the donation center on the agreed-upon date and time.

Follow any instructions provided to drop off your donations. If there is no specific drop-off process, look for designated areas or ask a staff member for assistance.

Step 8: Obtain a receipt (optional)

- Some donation centers offer receipts

for tax purposes. If you require a receipt, ask a staff member at the donation center if this is possible and provide the necessary information.

Step 9: Thank the donation center

- Show gratitude toward the donation center for accepting

your generous donations. Express your appreciation to the staff members who assisted you.

Step 10: Reflect on the impact

- Take a moment to reflect on the impact your donations can have on the lives of those in need. Knowing that your contribution can bring hope to someone's life can be a powerful motivator to continue supporting such causes in the future.

Summary: Tips for searching for employment, creating a resume, and utilizing job training programs or career centers specifically designed for homeless individuals.

Step 1: Assess your skills and interests

- Take some time to reflect on your skills, strengths, and interests. Consider what type of job you would enjoy and excel in. This self-reflection will help you focus your job search and find a meaningful career.

Step 2: Set job search goals

- Establish clear and realistic job search goals. Determine how many job applications you will submit each week, the number of interviews you aim to secure, and the industries or companies you want to target. Setting goals will keep you motivated and focused during the job hunt.

Step 3: Research job opportunities

- Utilize online job search engines and websites to find available positions. Make a list of the companies you are interested in and regularly check their career pages for any job postings. Additionally, network with professionals in your desired field and attend job fairs or networking events.

Step 4: Tailor your resume and cover letter to each job application

- Customize your resume and cover letter for each job application. Highlight relevant skills and experiences that align with the requirements of the job. Use action verbs and quantifiable achievements to showcase your abilities effectively.

Step 5: Prepare for interviews

- Research commonly asked interview

questions and formulate confident and concise answers. Practice mock interviews with a friend or family member to enhance your interview skills. Dress professionally, arrive early, and bring multiple copies of your resume and a list of references.

Step 6: Utilize job training programs and career centers

- Look for job training programs specifically designed for homeless individuals or individuals facing similar challenges. These programs can offer additional skills development, job coaching, and connections to employers who are open to hiring

individuals from
unique backgrounds.

**Step 7: Leverage
community resources
and support
networks**

- Reach out to local
community
organizations or
government agencies
that provide job
placement assistance
or resources for

homeless individuals.
These organizations
often have
partnerships with
employers who
understand the
unique challenges
faced by individuals
experiencing
homelessness.

**Step 8: Stay positive
and persistent**

- Job hunting can be challenging and may take time. Stay hopeful, maintain a positive attitude, and celebrate small victories along the way. Remember that every job application and interview is an opportunity to learn and improve your skills.

Step 9: Follow up and thank you notes

- After each interview, send a thank you email or note to express your appreciation for the opportunity to interview. This gesture showcases your professionalism and helps keep you top of mind for the hiring manager.

Step 10: Keep learning and growing

- Even if you secure a job, continue to seek opportunities for professional growth and skill development. Attend workshops, seminars, and online courses to continuously enhance your abilities, making yourself more marketable in the long run.

Remember, while job hunting can be challenging, maintaining hope and perseverance will ultimately lead you to your desired career path. Stay determined and

believe in your
abilities. Good luck!

Summary: An overview of government assistance programs, including welfare benefits, health insurance, and housing vouchers, and how to access them.

**Step 1: Understand the available

government
assistance programs

- Research and
familiarize yourself
with the various
government
assistance programs
that are relevant to
your needs, such as
welfare benefits,
health insurance, and
housing vouchers.

- Take note of the
eligibility criteria and

the benefits provided by each program.

Step 2: Determine your eligibility

- Review the eligibility criteria for each program and determine which ones you potentially qualify for.

- Gather any necessary

documentation or information required to support your eligibility, such as proof of income, identification documents, and household size.

Step 3: Assess your priorities and needs

- Prioritize your immediate needs and determine which

programs can provide the most assistance in those areas.

- For example, if you are in immediate need of affordable housing, focus on programs that offer housing vouchers or rental assistance.

Step 4: Seek assistance from

social service agencies

- Contact local social service agencies or community organizations that specialize in providing assistance with government programs.

- Explain your situation and ask for guidance on the best way to access the programs you are eligible for.

- Provide any necessary documentation or information they request to ensure a smooth application process.

Step 5: Complete applications accurately and thoroughly

- Obtain the necessary application forms for the programs you are applying for.

- Fill out each application completely and accurately, paying close attention to the specific requirements and details.

- Seek assistance from social service agencies if needed to

ensure your applications are correctly completed.

Step 6: Submit applications and follow up

- Submit your completed applications to the appropriate government offices or agencies, following their specific guidelines and deadlines.

- Keep copies of all submitted documents for reference and future communication.

- Follow up with the respective offices or agencies to ensure that your applications are being processed and to address any additional requirements or questions they may have.

Step 7: Stay informed and continue exploring options

- Stay informed about any updates or changes in the government assistance programs you are applying for.

- Research other
resources and
programs that may
be available to
support your needs,
such as local non-
profit organizations,
job training
programs, or
educational
opportunities.

- Stay hopeful and
persistent in your
search for assistance,
knowing that there
are resources

available to help you during challenging times.

Remember, navigating social services can be complex, but with determination and the support of social service agencies, you can access the assistance you need. Stay positive, seek

help when needed,
and continue to
explore potential
solutions.

Summary: Exploring daycare services, subsidized childcare, and community organizations that provide support for homeless parents.

Step 1: Research Daycare Services

- Start by using online resources to search for daycare services in your area.

- Look for reviews and ratings to gauge their quality and reputation.

- Consider factors such as location, operating hours, and cost.

Step 2: Visit Potential Daycare Centers

- Make a list of the daycare centers that

seem promising based on your research.

- Schedule visits to each center to get a firsthand look at their facilities and ask questions.

- Inquire about their curriculum, staff qualifications, safety measures, and any additional services provided.

Step 3: Check for Subsidized Childcare Options

- Look into subsidized childcare programs available in your area.

- Contact your local government agency or childcare resource and referral service to get more information.

- Find out the eligibility criteria, application process, and any required documentation.

Step 4: Research Community Organizations

- Seek out community organizations or non-profit agencies that provide support for homeless parents.

- Check if they offer childcare services or assistance programs.

- Contact them to discuss your situation and inquire about their offerings.

Step 5: Attend Parent Support Groups or Workshops

- Look for parent support groups or workshops in your community.

- These groups can provide valuable resources and emotional support for parents facing challenging circumstances.

- Participate in discussions and take advantage of any childcare-related

information
provided.

Step 6: Evaluate and Compare Options

- Review all the information and resources you have gathered.

- Consider the affordability, quality, proximity, and support services

provided by each
option.

- Prioritize the
options that align
with your needs and
values.

Step 7: Make
Decisions and Take
Action

- Once you have
evaluated and
compared all the

options, make a decision on which childcare option is the best fit for you and your child.

- Complete any necessary paperwork, such as enrollment forms or subsidy applications.

- Follow through with the necessary steps to secure a spot in your chosen daycare or childcare program.

Remember to stay hopeful throughout this process. With thorough research and exploration, you will be able to find the best childcare options and support for you and your child.

**Summary:
Encouraging self-care
practices, including
accessing mental
health services,
support groups, and
free or low-cost
health clinics.**

**Step 1: Educate
yourself about
mental health
resources in your
area**

- Research local
mental health clinics,
counseling centers,
and therapists that
offer free or low-cost
services.

- Familiarize yourself
with their services,
opening hours, and
contact information.

Step 2: Promote
mental health
awareness

- Share information about mental health services and resources with your friends, family, and community.

- Encourage open conversations about mental health and the importance of self-care.

Step 3: Organize mental health

workshops or
support groups

- Connect with local
organizations or
community centers
to arrange
workshops or
support groups
focused on self-care
and mental health.

- Invite professionals
or experts to share
insights and practical
tips on self-care
techniques.

Step 4: Utilize online resources

- **Explore reputable online platforms that provide information on mental health services or self-care practices.**

- **Share these resources on your social media profiles, blog, or community**

groups to reach a
wider audience.

Step 5: Advocate for accessible healthcare

- Voice your opinion on the importance of affordable mental health services in your community.

- Reach out to local representatives, organizations, or

government officials to advocate for accessible healthcare and funding for mental health support.

Step 6: Encourage regular self-care routines

- Emphasize the significance of self-care activities such as meditation, exercise, getting enough sleep, and engaging in hobbies.

- Provide resources and tips on incorporating these practices into daily life.

Step 7: Lead by example

- Take care of your own mental health

and practice self-care regularly.

- Share your experiences and the positive impact self-care has had on your well-being.

Step 8: Create a network of support

- Connect with individuals who share an interest in

promoting self-care and mental health.

- Establish a network where you can collaborate, share resources, and support each other in advocating for self-care.

Step 9: Evaluate and adjust your approach

- Regularly assess the effectiveness of your efforts to encourage self-care practices and access to mental health services.

- Make adjustments as needed and explore new strategies to reach a wider audience.

By following these steps, you can

contribute to encouraging self-care practices and promoting access to mental health services, support groups, and free or low-cost health clinics in a smart and effective way, to bring hope to those in need.

Summary: Discovering local organizations or support groups that cater to homeless individuals, where they can connect, share experiences, and find a sense of belonging.

Step 1: Research local organizations and support groups

1.1. Open a web browser and search for "local homeless organizations" or "homeless support groups" followed by the name of the city or area where you are located.

**1.2. Browse through the search results and make a list of organizations or groups that cater specifically to the needs of homeless individuals.

1.3. Take note of the organization's address, contact information, and any details regarding their programs or activities.

Step 2: Evaluate the organizations or support groups

2.1. Visit the websites or social media pages of the identified organizations or support groups.

2.2. Read about their mission, values, and the services they offer to homeless individuals.

**2.3. Look for testimonials or reviews from previous participants to get an idea of their experiences.

2.4. Consider factors such as the proximity to your location, available resources, and the compatibility with your personal goals and values.

Step 3: Contact the organization or support group

3.1. Shortlist the organizations or support groups that align with your needs and interests.

3.2. Find the contact information for each organization or group, such as email addresses or phone numbers.

**3.3. Reach out to them through the preferred method of contact and express your interest in joining or learning more about their programs.

3.4. Inquire about the application process, any requirements, and the availability of initial meetings or orientations.

Step 4: Attend meetings or orientations

4.1. Once you have received a response from the organization or support group, schedule a date to attend their meeting or orientation.

4.2. Prepare any necessary documents or forms as

instructed by the organization.

4.3. On the scheduled day, arrive at the specified location on time.

4.4. Participate actively and engage with others in the community.

4.5. Take note of any guidelines or expectations set by the organization or

support group during
the meeting.

Step 5: Establish connections and engage

5.1. After attending the initial meeting or orientation, introduce yourself to others and start building connections.

5.2. Share your experiences and listen to the experiences of others, expressing empathy and support.

5.3. Take advantage of any workshops, counseling services, or resources offered by the organization.

**5.4. Volunteer to contribute to the community by

offering your skills or time, if possible.

5.5. Attend regular meetings, events, and activities offered by the organization to stay connected and continuously build relationships.

Note: Building a sense of community takes time and effort. Be patient, persistent, and open-minded throughout the process. Remember, you are not alone – there are others experiencing similar challenges and seeking hope and belonging, just like you.

Summary: Identifying public spaces, such as community centers and homeless shelters, that offer shower and laundry facilities for those in need.

Introduction:

In times of uncertainty and hardship, finding access to basic facilities like showers

and laundry can bring hope and comfort. This chapter will guide you through the process of identifying public spaces that offer these resources, such as community centers and homeless shelters.

Step 1: Researching Public Resources

1. Start by conducting online research or contacting local organizations to find public spaces that offer shower and laundry facilities for those in need. Helpful resources may include:

   - Local government websites

   - Non-profit organizations

focused on helping
the homeless and
marginalized
communities

- Community
centers

- Homeless shelters

- Religious
organizations

Step 2: Evaluating Public Spaces

1. Once you have compiled a list of potential places, evaluate each one based on the following criteria:

   - Proximity to your location: Choose locations that are convenient to access.

   - Opening hours: Ensure the facility's operating hours align with your schedule.

- Facility conditions: Look for clean and well-maintained facilities to ensure your comfort and safety.

- Access requirements: Determine if any identification or prior registration is necessary to use the facilities.

Step 3: Contacting Facilities

1. Prioritize the facilities that meet your criteria and make a list of the contact information for each.

2. Reach out to these facilities via phone or email to gather further information. Inquire about the following:

- Availability of shower and laundry facilities: Ask if both services are offered or if they vary by location.

- Usage guidelines: Understand any rules or policies associated with the use of these facilities.

- Cost: Clarify if the services are offered for free or if they require a nominal fee or donation.

- Additional services: Inquire about any other resources available, such as toiletries, clean clothes, or support programs.

- COVID-19 precautions: Ask about any special measures implemented due to the ongoing pandemic.

Step 4: Creating a Schedule

1. Based on the information gathered, create a schedule that outlines the facilities available to you on different days and times.

2. Consider factors such as opening hours, proximity, and any other personal preferences or constraints.

Step 5: Utilizing Public Resources

1. Follow the schedule and visit the chosen facilities according to the

designated days and times.

2. Respect the rules and guidelines established by each facility.

3. If the facility requires registration or identification, ensure you have the necessary documentation with you.

4. Practice good hygiene and

cleanliness while using the facilities to maintain a safe and welcoming environment for everyone.

Conclusion:

Identifying public spaces that offer showers and laundry facilities is an essential step in providing hope and comfort during difficult times. By researching, evaluating, contacting, and utilizing these resources diligently, you can make the most of these public services designed to support individuals in need.

and **Rehabilitation Programs Summary: Highlighting vocational training programs, educational opportunities, and rehabilitation centers aimed at helping homeless individuals rebuild their lives.**

1. Research potential programs and centers: Begin by

gathering information on vocational training programs, educational opportunities, and rehabilitation centers specifically designed to assist homeless individuals in rebuilding their lives. Focus on finding programs that emphasize hope and provide the necessary resources and support to help individuals regain stability.

2. Select key programs and centers: From the research conducted, identify the most promising vocational training programs, educational opportunities, and rehabilitation

centers. Choose those that align with the theme of hope and offer a comprehensive support system.

3. Gather detailed information: Collect specific details about each chosen program or center. This information should include the type of

vocational training offered, the educational opportunities available, and the rehabilitation programs they provide. Pay attention to any success stories or testimonials that exemplify how the programs have helped individuals find hope and rebuild their lives.

4. Organize the information: Create a structured outline highlighting the vocational training programs, educational opportunities, and rehabilitation centers to be included in the chapter. Arrange the information in a logical order, such as grouping similar

programs together or prioritizing those with the most impactful success stories.

5. Write an introduction: Begin the chapter with an introduction that sets the stage by explaining the importance of life skills education and

rehabilitation programs for homeless individuals. Use this section to establish the overarching theme of hope and its significance in helping individuals in their journey towards rebuilding their lives.

6. Present the vocational training programs: Describe each vocational training program individually, including information on the skills taught, the duration of the training, any certifications or qualifications offered upon completion, and success stories of individuals who have benefited from the

program. Emphasize
how these programs
provide a fresh start
and ignite hope for a
better future.

7. Highlight
educational
opportunities:
Outline the
educational
opportunities
available to
homeless individuals

in the form of GED programs, scholarships, or access to community college. Discuss how these opportunities open doors to further education, creating a pathway out of homelessness and towards a new life filled with hope.

8. Explain the rehabilitation centers: Detail the rehabilitation centers that offer support services like mental health counseling, addiction recovery programs, job placement assistance, and housing support. Focus on success stories from individuals who have overcome challenges

with the help of these centers, showing how they provide hope and serve as a critical resource for rebuilding lives.

9. Provide additional resources: Include a list of additional resources such as support groups, job fairs, or mentorship

programs that can complement the vocational training programs, educational opportunities, and rehabilitation centers mentioned. These resources can act as supplementary tools for building hope and further empowering homeless individuals in their journey towards stability and self-sufficiency.

10. Conclusion: Wrap up the chapter by reiterating the importance of these life skills education and rehabilitation programs, reinforcing the message of hope and the positive impact they have on the lives of homeless individuals. Remind readers that everyone deserves a chance to rebuild their lives, and these programs offer them the support and resources they need to make lasting changes.

By following these step-by-step instructions, you can create a comprehensive and informative chapter

highlighting
vocational training
programs,
educational
opportunities, and
rehabilitation centers
that emphasize hope
in helping homeless
individuals rebuild
their lives.

Summary: Discovering different types of affordable or transitional housing options, including shelters, transitional housing programs, and low-income apartments.

Step 1: Conduct Research

1. Start by conducting thorough research on different

types of affordable or transitional housing options available in your area.

2. Look for shelters, transitional housing programs, and low-income apartments that offer hope for individuals seeking stable housing.

Step 2: Reach out to Local Organizations

1. Contact local organizations that specialize in providing housing assistance. These may include social service agencies, community centers, or non-profit organizations.

2. Inquire about any programs, resources, or support they offer

for individuals seeking affordable or transitional housing.

3. Ask for information on eligibility requirements, application processes, and any necessary documentation.

Step 3: Visit Shelters or Transitional Housing Programs

1. Visit local shelters or transitional housing programs to get a firsthand look at the facilities.

2. Speak with staff members or residents to gather information about the programs and their success rates in helping individuals

find permanent
housing.

3. Inquire about any
potential waiting lists
and the estimated
timeframe for
securing a spot in the
program.

Step 4: Explore Low-Income Apartments

1. Research low-
income apartments

in your area that offer affordable housing options.

2. Make a list of potential apartments and compare them based on factors such as rent, location, amenities, and eligibility requirements.

3. Contact the property managers or landlords to schedule visits to the

apartments that
interest you the
most.

4. During each visit,
assess the condition
of the apartments,
ask about waiting
lists, and inquire
about the application
process.

Step 5: Apply for Housing Options

1. Gather all necessary documentation required for the housing options you are interested in.

2. Complete and submit applications for shelters, transitional housing programs, and low-income apartments according to their respective guidelines.

3. Ensure that you have included all required information and supporting documents to avoid delays in the application process.

Step 6: Follow Up and Stay Persistent

1. Follow up with the organizations, shelters, and apartment managers

after submitting applications.

2. Inquire about the status of your application, ask about any additional steps that may be required, and express your continued interest.

3. Be patient and understand that the process of securing affordable or

transitional housing may take time.

Step 7: Seek Additional Support

1. If necessary, seek additional support from local organizations or social service agencies.

2. They may be able to provide resources

or assistance during your search for affordable or transitional housing.

3. Attend workshops or educational programs offered by these organizations to further enhance your life skills and increase your chances of finding suitable housing.

Step 8: Stay Hopeful and Persevere

1. Remember that the process of finding affordable or transitional housing can be challenging, but it's important to remain hopeful and persistent.

2. Continue searching for new opportunities and exploring different housing options.

3. Stay proactive in your efforts and utilize the resources available to you to increase your chances of finding the right housing solution.

Summary: Navigating the mental health system, accessing counseling and therapy services, and raising awareness about the importance of mental well-being while homeless.

**1. Research available mental health resources: Begin by researching the mental health services available in your area. This can include mental health clinics, community health centers, nonprofit organizations, and government-run programs. Look for resources that specifically cater to individuals who are homeless or have limited resources.

2. Make a list of contact information: Create a list of contact information for the mental health services you have identified. This should include phone numbers, email addresses, and physical addresses.

3. Gather necessary documentation: Determine the documentation requirements for accessing mental health services. This may include identification documents, proof of address, and income verification. Gather these documents in advance to streamline the application process.

4. Make initial contact: Reach out to the mental health services on your list. Call or email them to express your interest in accessing mental health support. Provide them with any necessary information they may need, such as your name, contact details, and

background
information.

5. Schedule
appointments: Once
you have made initial
contact, schedule
appointments with
the mental health
services you have
reached out to. Be
prepared to discuss
your mental health
concerns during

these appointments, as it will help the professionals understand your needs.

6. Attend counseling or therapy sessions: Attend your scheduled counseling or therapy sessions. Be open and honest with your therapist or counselor, as they

can provide valuable support and guidance. Utilize these sessions to work through any emotional or psychological challenges you may be facing.

7. Explore support groups: In addition to individual counseling or therapy, consider

joining support groups. These groups can provide an opportunity to connect with others who have similar experiences and can offer support and encouragement.

8. Raise awareness about mental well-being: While homeless, you can

take steps to raise awareness about the importance of mental well-being within your community. Share your own experiences and struggles with others to shed light on the need for accessible mental health services for homeless individuals. Consider working with local advocacy groups or

community
organizations to
amplify your
message.

Remember,
navigating the
mental health system
can be challenging.
Don't hesitate to
reach out to other
support services,
such as social
workers, case

managers, or local outreach teams, who may be able to provide additional assistance and guidance.

Summary: Finding local organizations, treatment centers, and peer support groups for individuals struggling with substance abuse or addiction.

Step 1: Research local organizations, treatment centers, and peer support groups

- Start by using search engines to find local organizations, treatment centers, and peer support groups that specialize in substance abuse and addiction in your area.

- Look for resources that offer a comprehensive range of services, such as counseling, therapy, detoxification programs, and aftercare programs. Consider whether you or the person you are assisting require any specific treatment approaches or modalities.

Step 2: Check reviews and reputations

- Read reviews and testimonials from previous clients to get an idea of the quality of care and support these organizations, treatment centers, or support groups provide.

- Consider reaching out to people who have already attended or participated in these programs to get firsthand insights about their experiences.

- Check if the organizations or centers are accredited or certified by reputable bodies, which can indicate their adherence to industry standards.

Step 3: Contact the selected organizations and treatment centers

- Make a list of the organizations, treatment centers, and support groups that seem most appropriate based on your research.

- Contact them individually to gather more information about their programs, eligibility criteria, costs, insurance coverage, availability, and any necessary prerequisites.

- Be prepared to describe the specific needs, concerns, and goals of the individual seeking assistance, as this will help the organizations assess if they can provide suitable support.

Step 4: Consult professionals and seek recommendations

- Reach out to medical professionals, therapists, social workers, or addiction specialists, who can provide expert guidance and recommendations

based on their experiences and expertise.

- Explain the situation honestly and ask for their advice or suggestions on the best local resources to consider during this process.

- They may also be able to recommend professionals who can conduct assessments to better understand the severity of substance abuse and addiction, which can help determine the most appropriate course of action.

Step 5: Make a final selection and take action

- After considering all the information and recommendations, make a final decision based on what you believe will provide the best support and assistance for the individual struggling with substance abuse or addiction.

- Contact the chosen organization, treatment center, or support group to schedule an initial consultation or assessment, if required.

- Ensure that all necessary paperwork, such as insurance information, medical records, or identification documents, are prepared and readily available.

- Continue to offer encouragement and support to the individual during this process, as it can often be a

challenging and
emotional journey.

Remember, every
individual's situation
is unique, and the
smartest way to
approach finding
local resources for
substance abuse and
addiction is to
consider the specific
needs and
circumstances of the

person seeking
assistance.

Summary: Understanding healthcare options available to homeless individuals, such as free or low-cost clinics, mobile healthcare units, and public health departments.

Step 1: Research local resources

**Start by researching the healthcare

options available for homeless individuals in your area. Look for free or low-cost clinics, mobile healthcare units, and public health departments that provide services to those in need.

Step 2: Contact local shelters or homeless service organizations

Reach out to local shelters or homeless service organizations and ask for information about the healthcare services they provide or if they can recommend any healthcare resources specifically for the homeless. These organizations often have partnerships with healthcare providers and can

help connect you to
the right resources.

Step 3: Visit a public health department

If your research or contacts with shelters and service organizations have led you to a public health department, visit their office to inquire about the healthcare services they offer. Ask about any specific programs or clinics they have for homeless individuals and how to access those services.

Step 4: Look for mobile healthcare units

Find out if there are mobile healthcare units in your area

that specifically cater to the healthcare needs of homeless individuals. These units often visit different locations regularly, providing medical services on-site. Check their schedules and locations and plan to visit when they are near you.

Step 5: Determine eligibility and required documentation

Once you have identified potential healthcare providers, find out what eligibility criteria and documentation they require for access to their services. Some may ask for proof of homelessness or income, while others may have less stringent requirements. Prepare any necessary documents, such as identification, proof of income, or a letter from a shelter confirming your homelessness.

Step 6: Plan for transportation

Consider how you will get to the healthcare facilities or mobile units. If you don't have your own transportation, research public transportation options in your area or see if the healthcare providers offer any assistance with transportation for homeless individuals.

Step 7: Make an appointment or visit during designated hours

Once you have gathered all the necessary information and documentation, make an appointment if required, or note the designated hours of operation for the healthcare provider or mobile unit. Plan your visit accordingly to ensure you can receive the care you need.

Step 8: Utilize any additional services

While accessing healthcare services, inquire about any additional resources

available to
homeless individuals.
These may include
access to mental
health services,
substance abuse
treatment, social
worker assistance, or
referrals to other
support programs.

Step 9: Follow up and
maintain continuity
of care

If your healthcare needs require ongoing treatment, follow the provider's recommendations and schedule any necessary follow-up appointments. Ensure you maintain continuity of care by attending appointments, taking prescribed medications, and staying in touch with your healthcare provider to address any concerns or changes in your health.

By following these steps, you can maximize your access to healthcare options and improve your well-being as a homeless individual. Remember that hope is a powerful tool,

and by seeking out
and utilizing these
resources, you are
taking positive steps
towards building a
healthier future.

Summary: Sharing information on affordable public transportation options, discounted fares, and transportation programs specifically for homeless individuals.

Step 1: Research affordable public transportation options in your area

- Use online search engines or apps to find out about the different public transportation options available in your area.

- Look for buses, trains, trams, or other means of transport that offer lower fares or special discounts for certain groups of people.

- Make a list of all the affordable options you find, along with their schedules, routes, and fares.

Step 2: Check if there are any discounted fares available

- Contact the public transportation companies or visit their websites to inquire about any discounted fares they offer.

- Ask specifically about discounts for students, seniors, veterans, or low-income individuals.

- Take note of the requirements or documentation needed to be eligible for the discounted fares.

Step 3: Look for transportation programs for homeless individuals

- Search for local or national transportation programs specifically designed to assist homeless individuals in accessing affordable public transportation.

- Contact homeless shelters,

organizations, or social service agencies in your area to inquire about any transportation assistance programs they offer.

- Explore programs that may provide discounted or free bus passes, subway tokens, or other transportation vouchers.

Step 4: Apply for eligible transportation programs

- Once you have identified transportation programs for homeless individuals, gather all the necessary documents or identification required to apply.

- Fill out any required forms or applications accurately, ensuring that you provide all the necessary information.

- Submit your application to the relevant organization or agency and follow up on its status if necessary.

Step 5: Stay updated with changes and updates

- Keep track of any changes in the public transportation schedules, fares, or discounts by regularly checking the websites or contacting the transportation companies.

- Sign up for any available email

newsletters or notifications to receive updates directly to your inbox.

- Stay connected with local shelters or social service agencies to be informed about any new transportation assistance programs that may become available.

Step 6: Utilize the transportation resources wisely

- Plan your journeys and schedules effectively to make the most of the affordable transportation options that you have access to.

- Arrive at bus stops or train stations on

time to avoid missing your ride or having to wait for longer periods.

- Familiarize yourself with the routes and schedules so that you can plan your trips efficiently, minimizing travel time.

By following these steps, you can

navigate the world of public transportation in a smarter way, finding affordable options, discounted fares, and transportation programs catered specifically towards homeless individuals, bringing hope for a more accessible and convenient means of transportation.

Summary: Finding legal assistance and advocacy groups that can offer guidance on issues related to homelessness, such as eviction, discrimination, or accessing public benefits.

Step 1: Research Legal Aid and Advocacy Organizations

- Begin by researching legal aid and advocacy organizations that specifically focus on issues related to homelessness. Look for organizations that offer support in areas such as eviction, discrimination, or accessing public benefits.

- Use search engines or directories specialized in legal

aid services to find relevant organizations in your area.

Step 2: Check Availability and Contact Information

- Once you have identified potential legal aid and advocacy organizations, visit their websites or call their contact numbers to check their availability and determine the services they offer.

- Take note of their contact information, including phone numbers, emails, and office addresses.

Step 3: Gather Relevant Documents and Information

- Before reaching out to the organizations, gather any relevant documents and information related to your issue. This may include lease agreements, eviction notices, correspondence with relevant parties, or any proof of discrimination or denial of benefits.

- Having these documents readily

available will help
the legal aid
organizations
understand your
situation and provide
better assistance.

Step 4: Make Initial Contact

- Reach out to the
legal aid organization
you have identified
as the best fit for
your situation. This

can be done through a phone call or by sending an email with a concise summary of your issue and the desired help you are seeking.

- Provide your contact information and availability to schedule an appointment or receive guidance.

Step 5: Attend Appointments or Seek Remote Assistance

- Depending on the organization's availability and their preferred method of communication, attend any scheduled appointments either in-person or virtually.

- During these appointments, be prepared to present

your documents and provide more detailed information about your situation.

- Listen carefully to the advice or guidance offered by the legal aid professionals and ask questions whenever needed for clarification.

Step 6: Follow Their Recommendations

- After receiving guidance or legal advice, carefully consider and follow the recommendations provided by the legal aid organization.

- This may involve actions such as filing a legal complaint, gathering additional evidence, or applying for public assistance programs.

- If the organization suggests further legal representation, ask for recommendations or referrals to appropriate lawyers or legal clinics.

Step 7: Stay Informed and Maintain Communication

- Throughout the process, stay informed of any updates or changes in your case or situation.

- Maintain open lines of communication with the legal aid organization and promptly provide any requested information or updates.

- Follow up regularly to ensure that your case is progressing and to address any additional concerns that may arise.

Step 8: Seek Further Assistance if Necessary

- If you encounter difficulties or unresolved issues, don't hesitate to

seek further
assistance from
additional legal aid
organizations or
advocacy groups.

- They may offer
alternative
perspectives,
additional resources,
or potential solutions
to help you navigate
your legal challenges.

Step 9: Express Gratitude and Share Your Experience

- If the legal aid organization successfully helps you resolve your issue or provides valuable guidance, express your gratitude by thanking the professionals who assisted you.

- Consider sharing your positive

experience with others who might benefit from their services, either through word-of-mouth recommendations or by leaving reviews on their website, social media platforms, or legal aid directories.

Remember, every situation is unique,

and these steps are just general guidelines. Adjust them accordingly based on your specific circumstances and the available resources in your area.

Summary: Addressing the unique challenges faced by homeless veterans, including resources specifically tailored to their needs, such as VA programs and veteran support organizations.

Step 1: Understand the Needs of Homeless Veterans

- Conduct thorough research and gain a comprehensive understanding of the challenges homeless veterans face, such as mental health issues, lack of job opportunities, and limited access to healthcare.

Step 2: Connect with Local Veteran Support Organizations

- **Research and identify local veteran support organizations that specialize in addressing homelessness among veterans.**

- Reach out to these organizations and inquire about their programs and services specifically designed for homeless veterans.

Step 3: Utilize VA Programs

- Visit the official website of the U.S. Department of Veterans Affairs (VA) and explore the programs they have available to assist homeless veterans.

- Familiarize yourself with programs such as the Homeless Veterans Outreach, Supportive Services for Veteran Families (SSVF), and Healthcare for Homeless Veterans (HCHV).

Step 4: Educate Yourself on Eligibility Criteria

- Understand the eligibility criteria for each program and service, including income requirements, veteran status, and documentation needed to qualify for assistance.

- Make a list of the eligibility criteria for each program to better assist homeless veterans in determining which ones they qualify for.

Step 5: Establish Partnerships with Local Agencies

- Reach out to local agencies, including housing authorities, job training centers, and mental health facilities, and discuss the possibility of establishing partnerships to support homeless veterans.

- Collaborate with these agencies to create a network of resources and services that can maximize support for homeless veterans in your community.

Step 6: Raise Awareness

- Organize awareness campaigns to educate the community about the challenges faced by homeless veterans and the resources available to support them.

- Utilize various platforms like social

media, local
newspapers, and
community events to
spread the message
of hope and
encourage
participation.

Step 7: Provide Supportive Services

- Establish initiatives
to provide basic
necessities such as
food, clothing, and

shelter to homeless veterans.

- Partner with local businesses, churches, and community organizations to gather donations and resources to meet the immediate needs of homeless veterans.

Step 8: Empower Veterans with Skill-

Building Opportunities

- Collaborate with vocational training centers and job placement agencies to offer skill-building programs and employment opportunities specifically designed for homeless veterans.

- Help them develop marketable skills and

secure sustainable employment to ensure long-term stability.

Step 9: Monitor Progress and Adapt

- Continuously monitor the progress and effectiveness of the support programs and services being provided to homeless veterans.

- Regularly review and update strategies to adapt to changing circumstances and better address the needs of homeless veterans.

Remember, addressing the challenges faced by

homeless veterans requires a strong commitment and collaboration among various stakeholders in your community. By taking these steps, you can provide hope and support to those who have served our nation.

and **Scholarships**

Summary: Providing guidance on returning to school or accessing educational resources, including scholarships and grants specifically available to homeless individuals.

Step 1: Assessing Educational Goals

1. Determine your educational goals

and aspirations, keeping in mind your passion and interests. Knowing what you want to achieve educationally will help you focus your efforts and make informed decisions.

Step 2: Research Educational Options

1. Conduct comprehensive research on the educational institutions that align with your goals. Consider factors such as location, programs offered, reputation, and support services available for homeless individuals.

Step 3: Find Scholarships and Grants

1. Search for scholarships and grants specifically designed for homeless individuals. These can help you fund your education and alleviate financial burdens. Websites like Scholarships.com, Fastweb.com, and CollegeBoard.org

provide databases of
available
scholarships.

Step 4: Review Eligibility Criteria

1. Thoroughly review the eligibility criteria for each scholarship or grant you locate, making sure you meet all the requirements. Some scholarships may

require you to have a certain GPA or financial need.

Step 5: Gather Required Documents

1. Collect all the necessary documents to apply for scholarships and grants. These may include proof of homelessness, academic transcripts,

essays, letters of recommendation, and financial statements.

Step 6: Draft Personal Statements and Essays

**1. Prepare personal statements and essays that highlight your experiences, challenges overcome, and aspirations in the context of being homeless. Emphasize your resilience, determination, and how education plays a role in your hope for a better future.

Step 7: Complete Application Forms

1. Fill out the application forms for each scholarship or grant carefully and

accurately. Pay attention to details and deadlines, ensuring you submit all required information.

Step 8: Submit Applications

1. Submit your completed applications before the specified deadlines. Keep

copies of everything you send, including confirmation emails or mail receipts, for your records.

Step 9: Follow Up on Application Status

1. Contact the scholarship or grant organizations to inquire about the status of your application. Be

proactive and reach out for updates, but also be patient as it may take some time for a response.

Step 10: Plan for Additional Funding

1. Consider alternative funding options, such as federal aid (FAFSA), private loans, or work-study

programs, to supplement your scholarships and grants. Explore all available resources to maximize financial support for your education.

Remember, accessing education and scholarships requires perseverance and patience. Keep your hope alive and maintain a positive attitude throughout the process. Don't hesitate to seek guidance from educational counselors or community organizations specializing in assisting homeless individuals with educational endeavors.

Summary: Discovering vocational training programs, apprenticeships, and skill-building initiatives that can help homeless individuals gain employment opportunities.

Step 1: Research local vocational training programs

- Start by researching local vocational training programs that cater to the needs of homeless individuals. Look for programs that offer skills training in industries with good employment prospects, such as construction, hospitality, healthcare, or information technology.

Step 2: Identify apprenticeship opportunities

- Once you have a list of potential vocational training programs, look for apprenticeship opportunities within those programs. Apprenticeships provide a combination of on-the-job training and classroom instruction, allowing individuals to gain practical skills and industry-specific knowledge while earning a wage.

Step 3: Consider skill-building initiatives

- Alongside vocational training programs and

apprenticeships, explore skill-building initiatives specifically designed for homeless individuals. These initiatives may offer a range of workshops, courses, or certifications to enhance individuals' existing skill sets or develop new ones.

Step 4: Connect with local homeless shelters or support organizations

- Reach out to local homeless shelters or support organizations to gather more information and assistance in identifying relevant training programs, apprenticeships, and skill-building initiatives. They may

have established
partnerships or
resources that can
help in this process.

Step 5: Assess eligibility requirements and application procedures

- Once you have identified potential programs, apprenticeships, and skill-building initiatives, carefully review their eligibility requirements and application procedures. Note any specific criteria, such as age limits, educational background, or work experience needed to participate.

Step 6: Prepare application materials

- Gather all the necessary documentation and materials required for the application process. This may include identification documents, educational certificates, resumes, references, and any other supporting documents as specified by each program.

Step 7: Submit applications and follow up

- Complete and submit the applications according to the instructions provided by each program. Keep copies of all submitted materials for reference. Additionally, consider following up with program coordinators or administrators to confirm the receipt of your application and inquire about the next steps in the selection process.

Step 8: Participate in interviews or assessments

- If shortlisted, you may be invited to undergo interviews or assessments as part of the selection process. Prepare for these interactions by researching common interview questions, practicing your responses, and showcasing your enthusiasm and

commitment to
obtaining the
necessary skills for
employment.

Step 9: Enroll in
chosen program or
initiative

- Once accepted into
a vocational training
program,
apprenticeship, or
skill-building
initiative, follow the

enrollment instructions provided. Attend all orientation sessions, complete any required paperwork, and familiarize yourself with the program structure, expectations, and schedules.

Step 10: Participate actively and stay committed

- Throughout the program, apprenticeship, or initiative, actively participate and engage in all learning activities. Demonstrate your commitment, ask questions, seek feedback, and take advantage of any additional resources or support services offered.

Step 11: Network and seek employment opportunities

- While in the program, take advantage of networking opportunities. Attend job fairs, industry events, or community gatherings where you can connect with potential employers or professionals in your desired field. Seek guidance from program mentors or coaches regarding job search strategies and utilize online job search platforms.

Step 12: Continued skill-building and growth

- After completing the program or apprenticeship, continue to reinforce and expand your skills through additional training, workshops, or certifications. Maintain a growth mindset and seek opportunities for career advancement or further education to enhance employment prospects and achieve greater financial stability.

Remember, this is a general guide, and the specific steps and resources available may vary based on your location and circumstances. Stay

hopeful, determined,
and resilient in your
journey towards
gaining employment
opportunities
through skills
training programs.

Budgeting Summary: Emphasizing the significance of financial literacy and budgeting skills for homeless individuals, offering tips on managing money, accessing banking services, and avoiding financial pitfalls.

Step 1: Start by conducting research on the importance of financial literacy and budgeting for homeless individuals. Look for relevant articles, studies, or resources that highlight the benefits and strategies of managing money effectively.

Step 2: Create an outline for your chapter, organizing the information you gathered in a logical and coherent manner. Divide it into sections that address specific aspects of financial literacy and budgeting for homeless individuals.

Step 3: Begin the chapter with an introduction that outlines the importance of financial literacy and budgeting skills for homeless individuals. Explain the potential positive impact these skills can have on their lives and their ability to find hope and stability.

Step 4: In the first section, provide an overview of basic financial literacy concepts that are essential for homeless individuals. Include information on understanding financial terms, budgeting, and differentiating between needs and wants.

Step 5: In the next section, offer practical tips on how to manage money effectively, even with limited resources. Provide guidance on creating a budget, tracking expenses, and prioritizing spending to meet essential needs.

Step 6: Discuss the benefits and importance of accessing banking services for homeless individuals. Explain how having a bank account can help them save money, establish a financial identity, and access financial tools and resources.

Step 7: Address common financial pitfalls that homeless individuals may encounter, such as predatory lending, scams, and high-interest loans. Provide advice on how to identify and avoid these pitfalls to protect their financial well-being.

Step 8: Include real-life stories or case studies of homeless individuals who have successfully improved their financial situation through financial literacy and budgeting. These stories can serve as inspiration and provide tangible examples of how hope can be restored

through effective money management.

Step 9: Wrap up the chapter with a conclusion that summarizes the main points and emphasizes the ongoing importance of financial literacy and budgeting for homeless individuals. Provide additional

resources or references for further reading or assistance.

Step 10: Proofread and edit your chapter carefully, ensuring that the information is accurate, clear, and well-organized. Consider seeking feedback from others to gain different perspectives and refine your content.

Step 11: Incorporate any feedback or revisions into your chapter, making sure the information flows smoothly and aligns with the theme of hope.

Step 12: Once you are satisfied with the final version of your chapter, format it appropriately according to the guidelines provided by the publishing platform or the intended audience. Ensure it is well-presented and visually appealing.

Step 13: Submit your chapter to the appropriate publication, considering online platforms, academic journals, or relevant organizations that focus on homelessness and financial literacy.

Step 14: After completing the

submission, take a moment to celebrate your accomplishment and share your work with others who may benefit from the information and insights you have provided.

Summary: Discussing the importance of maintaining physical health while homeless, including tips on staying active, accessing healthcare resources, and overcoming barriers to healthcare.

Step 1: Staying Active

1. Find a local park or community center that offers free or low-cost exercise programs. Look for options such as yoga, walking groups, or outdoor fitness classes.

2. Engage in regular physical activities that can easily be done without any equipment, such as walking, jogging, or cycling.

3. Utilize online resources or smartphone apps that provide free workout routines that can be done in small spaces, such as bodyweight exercises or yoga sessions.

4. Incorporate physical activity into daily routines, such as taking the stairs instead of the elevator or doing household chores

that require
movement.

Step 2: Accessing Healthcare Resources

1. Research local
healthcare clinics or
community health
centers that offer
services specifically
for individuals who

are homeless or low-income.

2. Make inquiries about eligibility requirements, as some clinics may require proof of homelessness or low income to avail services.

3. Utilize resources like free health fairs or outreach programs conducted by local hospitals or

non-profit organizations, which often offer free check-ups, vaccinations, and general healthcare services.

4. Seek out mobile healthcare clinics that specifically serve homeless communities. These clinics often provide primary care, mental health services, and basic medications

directly on the streets.

Step 3: Overcoming Barriers to Healthcare

1. Contact local homeless shelters or organizations that specialize in homeless assistance.

They might have social workers or case managers who can help navigate the healthcare system and assist with appointment scheduling and transportation.

2. Utilize online healthcare portals or apps to schedule appointments, access medical records, and communicate with

healthcare
professionals.

3. Research healthcare resources that provide assistance with health insurance enrollment or eligibility for government subsidized healthcare programs.

4. Stay updated with local news or community events

where free health screenings, immunizations, or specialized healthcare services might be offered.

Remember, everyone's situation is unique, so it's crucial to tailor these steps to personal circumstances. Additionally, building a support network and utilizing local resources can greatly aid in navigating the healthcare system while homeless.

Summary: Encouraging resilience and hope in the face of homelessness, sharing stories of individuals who have successfully transitioned out of homelessness, and providing inspiration for a brighter future.

Step 1: Start by researching and

gathering stories of individuals who have successfully transitioned out of homelessness. Look for stories that showcase resilience, determination, and hope.

Step 2: Organize the stories into a format that is easy to understand and visually appealing. Consider using headings, bullet points, and images to make the information more engaging.

Step 3: Include statistics and facts about homelessness and the success rates of individuals who have transitioned out of it. This will provide a context for the stories and emphasize the importance of hope and resilience.

Step 4: Add quotes and testimonials from individuals who have overcome homelessness, highlighting the emotions and mindset that helped them through their journey. Encourage readers to find hope and inspiration in these stories.

Step 5: Incorporate interactive elements such as links to resources and support organizations for homeless individuals.

This will provide practical help and options for readers who are seeking a way out of homelessness.

Step 6: Conclude the chapter with a call to action, encouraging readers to believe in their own resilience and to seek support and resources to help

them on their path to
a brighter future.

**Step 7: Proofread
and edit the chapter,
ensuring that the
content is clear,
concise, and free of
errors.**

**Step 8: Consider
adding visual**

elements such as graphics, charts, or infographics to enhance the visual appeal and comprehension of the chapter.

Step 9: Seek feedback from others, such as colleagues or individuals who have experienced homelessness themselves, to ensure that the chapter effectively conveys the theme of hope and offers valuable insights.

Step 10: Once finalized, share the chapter through appropriate channels such as a book, website, or

presentation, making
sure to reach the
target audience who
could benefit from
the message of
resilience and hope
in the face of
homelessness.

Please share your
story with the world.
-J. September-06-
2023-0704.
Townsend Atomics.

www.ingramcontent.com/pod-product-compliance
Lightning Source LLC
Chambersburg PA
CBHW070919260726

48661CB00003B/753